~A BINGO BOOK~

New York
Bingo Book

COMPLETE BINGO GAME IN A BOOK

EXCELSIOR

Written By Rebecca Stark

ISBN 978-0-87386-525-8

Educational Books 'n' Bingo

Printed in the U.S.A.

DIRECTIONS

INCLUDED:

List of Terms

Templates for Additional Terms and Clues

2 Clues per Term

30 Unique Bingo Cards

Markers

1. **Either cut apart the book or make copies of ALL the sheets. You might want to make an extra copy of the clue sheets to use for introduction and review. Keep the sheets in an envelope for easy reuse.**

2. Cut apart the call cards with terms and clues.

3. Pass out one bingo card per student. There are enough for a class of 30.

4. Pass out markers. You may cut apart the markers included in this book or use any other small items of your choice.

5. Decide whether or not you will require the entire card to be filled. Requiring the entire card to be filled provides a better review. However, if you have a short time to fill, you may prefer to have them do the just the border or some other format. Tell the class before you begin what is required.

6. There are 50 terms. Read the list before you begin. If there are any terms that have not been covered in class, you may want to read to the students the term and clues before you begin.

7. There is a blank space in the middle of each card. You can instruct the students to use it as a free space or you can write in answers to cover terms not included. Of course, in this case you would create your own clues. (Templates provided.)

8. Shuffle the cards and place them in a pile. Two or three clues are provided for each term. If you plan to play the game with the same group more than once, you might want to choose a different clue for each game. If not, you may choose to use more than one clue.

9. Be sure to keep the cards you have used for the present game in a separate pile. When a student calls, "Bingo," he or she will have to verify that the correct answers are on his or her card AND that the markers were placed in response to the proper questions. Pull out the cards that are on the student's card keeping them in the order they were used in the game. Read each clue as it was given and ask the student to identify the correct answer from his or her card.

10. If the student has the correct answers on the card AND has shown that they were marked in response to the *correct questions,* then that student is the winner and the game is over. If the student does not have the correct answers on the card OR he or she marked the answers in response to *the wrong questions,* then the game continues until there is a proper winner.

11. If you want to play again, reshuffle the cards and begin again.

Have fun!

TERMS INCLUDED

Adirondack Upland

Apple(s)

Albany

Appalachian Upland

Atlantic Coastal Plain

Beaver

Border

Buffalo

Climate (-ic)

Coney Island

Constitution

Cooperstown

County (-ies)

Dairy Products

Ellis Island

Empire State

Erie Canal

Executive Branch

Millard Fillmore

Flag

Fort Ticonderoga

Great Lakes Plain

Henry Hudson

Hudson Mohawk Lowland

Hudson River

Industry (-ies)

Iroquois

Washington Irving

John Jay

Judicial Branch

Kingston

Lake George

Lake Placid

Legislative Branch

St. Lawrence-Champlain Lowland

Motto

New England Upland

New Netherland

New York City

Niagara Falls

River(s)

Franklin Delano Roosevelt

Theodore Roosevelt

Snapping Turtle

Statue of Liberty

Thousand Islands

United Nations

Martin Van Buren

Giovanni da Verrazano

West Point

Additional Terms

Choose as many additional terms as you would like and write them in the squares. Repeat each as desired.
Cut out the squares and randomly distribute them to the class.
Instruct the students to place their square on the center space of their card.

New York Bingo

Clues for Additional Terms

Write three clues for each of your additional terms.

_____	_____
1.	1.
2.	2.
3.	3.
_____	_____
1.	1.
2.	2.
3.	3.
_____	_____
1.	1.
2.	2.
3.	3.

New York Bingo

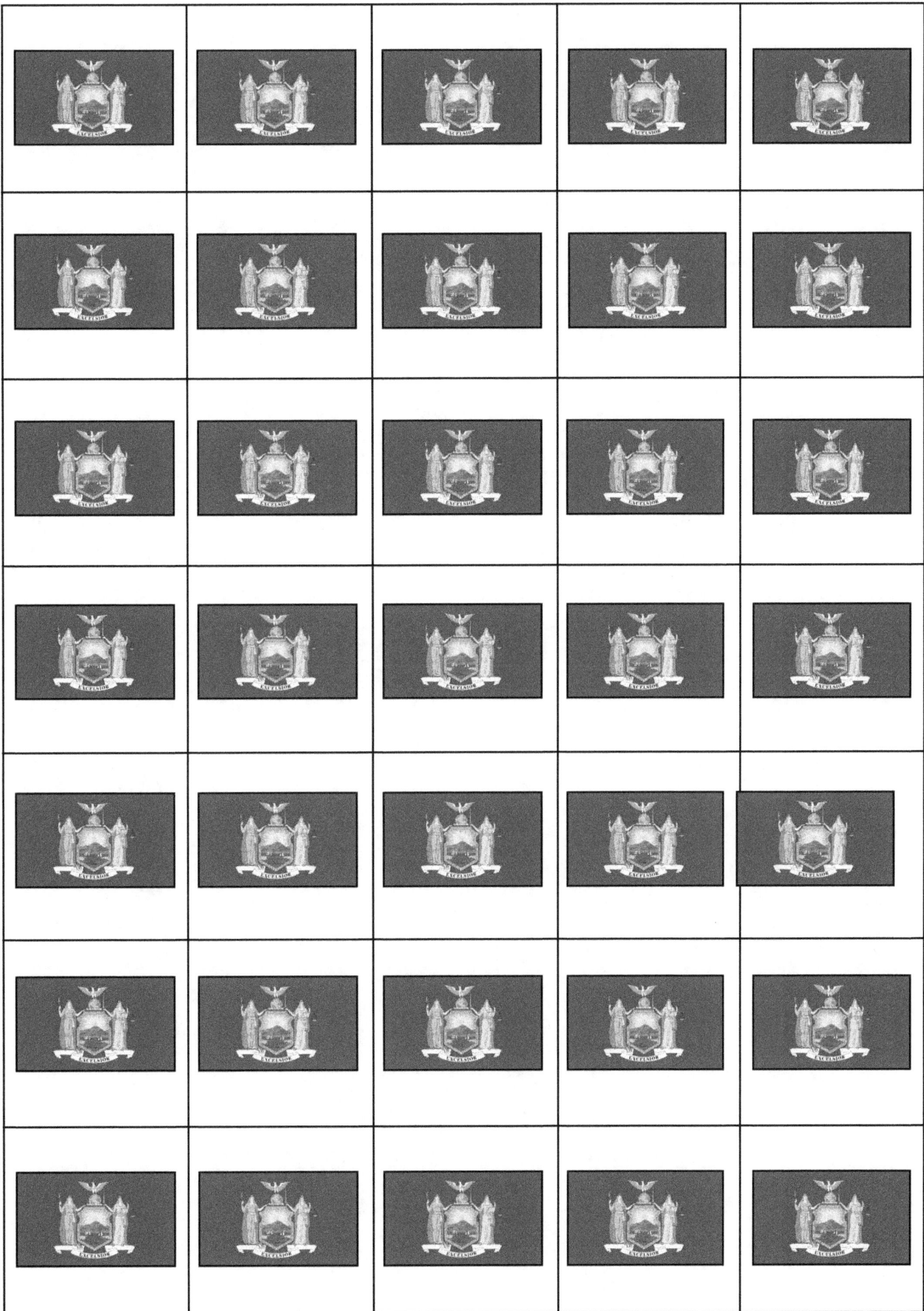

Adirondack Upland 1. The ___ is south of the St. Lawrence-Champlain Lowland. There are more than 2,000 lakes in this geographic region, including Lake Placid and Lake Champlain. 2. Mt. Marcy, the highest mountain in New York, is in the ___ region.	**Apple(s)** 1. The ___ is the state fruit. 2. New York is a leading fruit and vegetable producer. ___ are the most important fruit crop. Grapes are also very important.
Albany 1. ___ is the capital of New York State. 2. ___ is on the west bank of the Hudson River. It became the state capital in 1797.	**Appalachian Upland** 1. The ___ region is west of the Hudson River. It extends westward toward Lake Erie. Binghamton, Ithaca, and Jamestown are in this region. 2. Also known as the Allegheny Plateau, the ___ includes the Catskill Mountains and the Finger Lakes.
Atlantic Coastal Plain 1. The ___ is a low, relatively flat plain near the Atlantic Ocean. 2. The ___ region includes Long Island and a small portion of Staten Island.	**Beaver** 1. The ___ is the state mammal. 2. This animal's dam-building activities are important to natural water flow and erosion control.
Border 1. These states ___ New York: Vermont, Massachusetts, Connecticut, New Jersey, and Pennsylvania. New York also has an international ___: Canada. 2. Lake Ontario, Lake Erie, Lake Champlain, and the Atlantic Ocean all ___ New York.	**Buffalo** 1. ___ is the second most populous city in the state. It is an important industrial center. 2. ___ grew quickly after the opening of the Erie Canal in 1825. ___ was its western terminus.
Climate (-ic) 1. New York generally has a humid continental ___, but there is a lot of variation. 2. There are 3 main ___ regions: the southeastern lowlands, which have the warmest temperatures; the uplands, where winters are cold and summers cool; and the snow belt along the Great Lakes Plain.	**Coney Island** 1. This beach resort and amusement area was once an outer barrier island, but was partially connected to the mainland by landfill. 2. Three rides at ___ are in the National Register of Historic Places: Wonder Wheel, a steel Ferris wheel, The Cyclone, a wooden roller coaster; and the Parachute Jump.

Constitution
1. New York was one of the original 13 states. It ratified the ___ on July 26, 1788.
2. New York became the 11th state when it ratified the ___.

Cooperstown
1. ___ is home to the Baseball Hall of Fame and Museum.
2. ___ was named after Judge William Cooper, not his famous son, author James Fenimore Cooper.

County (-ies)
1. There are 62 ___ in New York State.
2. Each of New York City's 5 boroughs is also a ___.

Dairy
1. ___ products are the most important agricultural products in terms of revenue.
2. ___ New York is a leading producer of ___ products, especially milk, which is the state beverage.

Ellis Island
1. ___ is in Upper New York Bay. It was the gateway for millions of immigrants from 1892 to 1954.
2. ___ was made part of the Statue of Liberty National Monument in 1965; its museum of immigration opened in 1990.

Empire State
1. "The ___" is the state's nickname.
2. The ___ Building is a 102-story skyscraper located in Midtown Manhattan.

Erie Canal
1. The ___ links the waters of Lake Erie in the west to the Hudson River in the east.
2. The ___ was an engineering marvel of its day. Opponents to its construction called it "Clinton's Big Ditch" in reference to Governor Dewitt Clinton.

Executive Branch
1. The ___ of government enforces laws. It comprises the governor, the comptroller, the attorney general, and several agencies.
2. The governor is head of the ___ of state government. George Clinton was the first governor.
The present-day governor is [fill in].

Millard Fillmore
1. ___ was born in Locke Township, now Summerhill. He became President upon the death of President Zachary Taylor.
2. ___ was the 13th President of the United States, serving from 1850 to 1853.

Flag
1. The state coat of arms is on the state ___.
2. The state ___ has a field of dark blue.

New York Bingo

Fort Ticonderoga 1. Ethan Allen and Benedict Arnold co-commanded an attack on ___. It was one of the first American victories of the Revolution. 2. Fort Carillon was renamed ___. It is on Lake Champlain.	**Great Lakes Plain** 1. The ___ covers the northwestern part of the state. It runs from Lake Erie to Lake Ontario. 2. Buffalo, Rochester, and Syracuse are all in this geographic area.
Henry Hudson 1. This Englishman explored the area around present-day New York City for the Dutch in the early 17th century. This laid the foundation for Dutch colonization of the region. 2. His ship was called the *Half Moon*. A river, a strait, and a bay were named in his honor.	**Hudson Mohawk Lowland** 1. The ___ is shaped like the letter "Y." It covers most of the Hudson River Valley, including the historic colonial sites of Philipsburg Manor and Van Cortlandt Manor. 2. Albany, Utica and other port cities are in the ___ geographic region.
Hudson River 1. The ___ is named after Henry Hudson, an Englishman sailing for the Dutch East India Company, who explored it in 1609. 2. The ___ flows from north to south through eastern New York State, It serves as part of the political boundary between New York and New Jersey.	**Industry (-ies)** 1. Finance, international trade, fashion, communications, and publishing are important ___. 2. Tourism is an important ___.
Iroquois 1. Most of the native peoples of New York State were ___. 2. The ___ League comprised the Mohawk, Oneida, Onondaga, Cayuga, and Seneca nations. In 1722 the Tuscarora nation joined.	**Washington Irving** 1. ___'s home in Sunnyside is a popular tourist attraction. It is in Tarrytown in the Hudson Valley. 2. ___ is best known for his short stories "The Legend of Sleepy Hollow" and "Rip Van Winkle."
John Jay 1. ___ was the nation's first Chief Justice of the Supreme Court. 2. ___ resigned from the Supreme Court to become New York's second governor.	**Judicial Branch** 1. The ___ interprets what our laws mean and makes decisions about the laws and those who break them. 2. The ___ is made up of several courts, the highest of which is the state Supreme Court.

Kingston 1. ___ was the first capital of the state. 2. The farmers near ___ provided Washington's troops with wheat and other food supplies. ___ became known as "the Breadbasket of the Revolution."	**Lake George** 1. Fort William Henry is at the southern end of ___. 2. ___ is located in the southeastern Adirondack State Park in Warren County. It is nicknamed "Queen of American Lakes."
Lake Placid 1. ___ is in the Adirondacks in Essex County. ___, Saranac Lake, and Tupper Lake make up what is known as the Tri-Lakes Region. 2. ___ hosted the Winter Olympics in 1932 and 1980.	**Legislative Branch** 1. The ___ comprises the State Senate and the State Assembly. 2. The ___ makes the laws.
St. Lawrence-Champlain Lowland 1. The ___ geographic region connects the Atlantic Ocean and the Great Lakes. 2. The ___ is the northernmost geographic region. The Thousand Islands are in this region.	**Motto** 1. Beneath the shield on the state coat of arms is the ___ "Excelsior." 2. The state ___, "Excelsior," means "Ever upward."
New England Upland 1. The geographic region known as the ___ is east of the Hudson River. 2. The ___ geographic region extends eastward into Massachusetts and Connecticut. It extends southward across the lower Hudson Valley into Pennsylvania.	**New Netherland** 1. The English took over of the area that had been called ___ in 1664. 2. New Amsterdam was the capital of ___. The English renamed ___ it New York to honor the Duke of York.
New York City 1. ___ was the national capital at various times between 1785 and 1790. Its nickname is "The Big Apple." 2. ___ is the most populous city in the United States. It comprises 5 boroughs: the Bronx, Brooklyn, Queens, Manhattan, and Staten Island.	**Niagara Falls** 1. ___ is the collective name for the Horseshoe Falls, the American Falls, and Bridal Veil Falls. 2. Its combined falls form the highest flow rate of any waterfall in the world. Horseshoe Falls is the most powerful waterfall in North America.

New York Bingo

River(s)	Franklin Delano Roosevelt
1. The Hudson, the Genesee, the Allegheny, and the Mohawk are important ___ of the state. 2. Nyack, West Point, and Rhineback are a few of the towns along the Hudson ___.	1. ___ was born in Hyde Park on January 30, 1882. His home there is now a National Historic Site. 2. ___ was the 32th United States President. He is the only President elected to more than 2 terms.
Theodore Roosevelt 1. ___ was born in New York City on October 27, 1858. He formed the Rough Riders, a volunteer cavalry regiment that fought in Cuba during the Spanish-American War. 2. ___ became the 26th President in 1901 when President William McKinley was assassinated.	**Snapping Turtle** 1. The common ___ is the state reptile. 2. The ___ has a relatively small shell that does not cover its limbs or tail.
Statue of Liberty 1. This monument on Liberty Island was a gift from the people of France. 2. The ___ represents Libertas, the Roman goddess of freedom. Her tablet represents the law, and the broken chain at her feet represents freedom.	**Thousand Islands** 1. The ___ is an archipelago in the St. Lawrence River along the U.S.-Canadian border. 2. Some of the ___ are part of Canada; they are in the province of Ontario. Some are part of the United States; they are in the state of New York.
United Nations 1. The headquarters of this international organization are in New York City. 2. Many diplomats from foreign countries come to New York City because the ___ is located there.	**Martin Van Buren** 1. This New Yorker served as President from 1837 to 1841. He had previously been vice-president under President Andrew Jackson. 2. ___ was the 8th United States President. He was the first President born a citizen of the United States.
Giovanni da Verrazano 1. ___ was an Italian navigator who sailed for France. He explored the northeast coast of North America, including New York Bay. 2. The suspension bridge that spans New York Harbor, connecting Brooklyn and Staten Island, was named for him.	**West Point** 1. The United States Military Academy is located in ___, New York. 2. ___ was a fortified site during the Revolutionary War. The military academy there was established in 1802.
New York Bingo	© Barbara M. Peller

New York Bingo

New Netherland	Adirondack Upland	Albany	Millard Fillmore	Atlantic Coastal Plain
Erie Canal	Apple(s)	Martin Van Buren	Judicial Branch	River(s)
United Nations	John Jay		St. Lawrence-Champlain Lowland	Giovanni da Verrazano
Thousand Islands	Niagara Falls	Statue of Liberty	Washington Irving	Lake George
Legislative Branch	Great Lakes Plain	County (-ies)	Theodore Roosevelt	Hudson Mohawk Lowland

New York Bingo: Card No. 1

New York Bingo

Thousand Islands	United Nations	Henry Hudson	New York City	Iroquois
Lake George	Ellis Island	Buffalo	Niagara Falls	Lake Placid
Dairy Products	Great Lakes Plain		Hudson River	Statue of Liberty
Motto	New England Upland	John Jay	West Point	Atlantic Coastal Plain
River(s)	Martin Van Buren	County (-ies)	Erie Canal	Theodore Roosevelt

New York Bingo: Card No. 2

New York Bingo

Great Lakes Plain	Statue of Liberty	Ellis Island	Washington Irving	United Nations
Lake George	Apple(s)	Climate (-ic)	Adirondack Upland	Fort Ticonderoga
Niagara Falls	Martin Van Buren		Lake Placid	Appalachian Upland
John Jay	Dairy Products	Legislative Branch	Motto	Henry Hudson
Theodore Roosevelt	Coney Island	County (-ies)	West Point	Iroquois

New York Bingo

John Jay	Lake Placid	Albany	Coney Island	Iroquois
Kingston	Border	Adirondack Upland	New York City	United Nations
St. Lawrence-Champlain Lowland	Motto		Hudson Mohawk Lowland	Millard Fillmore
Statue of Liberty	Apple(s)	Martin Van Buren	County (-ies)	Buffalo
Constitution	River(s)	Beaver	Theodore Roosevelt	Giovanni da Verrazano

New York Bingo

River(s)	Atlantic Coastal Plain	Niagara Falls	Buffalo	Coney Island
Kingston	Statue of Liberty	Climate (-ic)	Hudson River	Apple(s)
Albany	Giovanni da Verrazano		Judicial Branch	Flag
Hudson Mohawk Lowland	Iroquois	New Netherland	West Point	Cooperstown
Ellis Island	County (-ies)	United Nations	John Jay	St. Lawrence-Champlain Lowland

New York Bingo

Appalachian Upland	Lake Placid	Henry Hudson	Iroquois	Giovanni da Verrazano
Washington Irving	Niagara Falls	Cooperstown	Adirondack Upland	United Nations
New York City	Constitution		Border	Hudson River
County (-ies)	Legislative Branch	West Point	Beaver	Albany
Lake George	Buffalo	New Netherland	St. Lawrence-Champlain Lowland	Empire State

New York Bingo

New Netherland	Lake Placid	Flag	Statue of Liberty	Ellis Island
Lake George	Iroquois	Great Lakes Plain	Apple(s)	Kingston
Giovanni da giovanni da verrazano	Millard Fillmore		Hudson River	Border
John Jay	Motto	Climate (-ic)	Thousand Islands	Dairy Products
County (-ies)	Coney Island	West Point	Beaver	Appalachian Upland

New York Bingo

St. Lawrence-Champlain Lowland	Lake Placid	Executive Branch	Washington Irving	Border
Kingston	Albany	New York City	Giovanni da Verrazano	Buffalo
Empire State	Coney Island		Iroquois	Atlantic Coastal Plain
Theodore Roosevelt	John Jay	Thousand Islands	Constitution	Motto
Martin Van Buren	County (-ies)	Beaver	Niagara Falls	Lake George

New York Bingo: Card No. 8

New York Bingo

Hudson River	Ellis Island	Great Lakes Plain	Empire State	Coney Island
Constitution	Iroquois	St. Lawrence-Champlain Lowland	Niagara Falls	Lake Placid
Fort Ticonderoga	New Netherland		Apple(s)	Executive Branch
Cooperstown	Atlantic Coastal Plain	Legislative Branch	Judicial Branch	Flag
Motto	West Point	Climate (-ic)	Thousand Islands	Hudson Mohawk Lowland

New York Bingo

Thousand Islands	Washington Irving	Border	New York City	Empire State
Giovanni da Verrazano	Buffalo	Adirondack Upland	Apple(s)	Iroquois
Coney Island	Lake Placid		Millard Fillmore	Dairy Products
Legislative Branch	Hudson Mohawk Lowland	Cooperstown	West Point	Fort Ticonderoga
Climate (-ic)	Lake George	Henry Hudson	River(s)	St. Lawrence-Champlain Lowland

New York Bingo

Appalachian Upland	Lake Placid	Niagara Falls	Cooperstown	Lake George
Executive Branch	Fort Ticonderoga	Judicial Branch	Hudson River	Adirondack Upland
Kingston	Iroquois		Henry Hudson	Great Lakes Plain
Climate (-ic)	United Nations	West Point	Coney Island	Thousand Islands
Constitution	County (-ies)	New Netherland	Beaver	Ellis Island

New York Bingo: Card No. 11

New York Bingo

Ellis Island	Atlantic Coastal Plain	Fort Ticonderoga	Washington Irving	Hudson River
Great Lakes Plain	Lake George	Albany	Beaver	Apple(s)
New Netherland	Flag		Giovanni da Verrazano	New York City
County (-ies)	Motto	Iroquois	Thousand Islands	Kingston
Lake Placid	Executive Branch	Coney Island	Constitution	Buffalo

New York Bingo

Cooperstown	Atlantic Coastal Plain	Appalachian Upland	Fort Ticonderoga	Giovanni da Verrazano
Albany	Executive Branch	Iroquois	Hudson River	Dairy Products
Washington Irving	Buffalo		Great Lakes Plain	Flag
St. Lawrence-Champlain Lowland	West Point	Border	Coney Island	Thousand Islands
County (-ies)	Hudson Mohawk Lowland	Beaver	New Netherland	Judicial Branch

New York Bingo: Card No. 13

New York Bingo

Erie Canal	Iroquois	Niagara Falls	Hudson River	Constitution
Buffalo	New Netherland	Fort Ticonderoga	Apple(s)	Lake Placid
Cooperstown	Millard Fillmore		Henry Hudson	Climate (-ic)
Hudson Mohawk Lowland	West Point	Coney Island	Border	Appalachian Upland
County (-ies)	New York City	Dairy Products	Lake George	St. Lawrence-Champlain Lowland

New York Bingo

Judicial Branch	Hudson River	Niagara Falls	Ellis Island	Washington Irving
Appalachian Upland	Henry Hudson	Adirondack Upland	Albany	Constitution
Giovanni da Verrazano	New Netherland		United Nations	Lake Placid
County (-ies)	Fort Ticonderoga	Executive Branch	West Point	Cooperstown
Lake George	Motto	Beaver	Empire State	Great Lakes Plain

New York Bingo: Card No. 15

New York Bingo

Border	Fort Ticonderoga	Executive Branch	Empire State	New England Upland
New York City	Dairy Products	Flag	Kingston	Millard Fillmore
Cooperstown	Atlantic Coastal Plain		Giovanni da Verrazano	Great Lakes Plain
John Jay	Buffalo	County (-ies)	Judicial Branch	Thousand Islands
Constitution	Snapping Turtle	Beaver	Motto	Lake Placid

New York Bingo

Climate (-ic)	Franklin Delano Roosevelt	Industry (-ies)	Fort Ticonderoga	Erie Canal
Judicial Branch	Constitution	West Point	Millard Fillmore	Flag
Hudson River	St. Lawrence-Champlain Lowland		Snapping Turtle	Executive Branch
Hudson Mohawk Lowland	Lake George	Thousand Islands	Niagara Falls	Dairy Products
Legislative Branch	Cooperstown	Ellis Island	Washington Irving	Atlantic Coastal Plain

New York Bingo

Empire State	Coney Island	Buffalo	Cooperstown	New York City
Lake Placid	Climate (-ic)	Legislative Branch	Giovanni da Verrazano	Constitution
Hudson River	Dairy Products		Industry (-ies)	Albany
Atlantic Coastal Plain	Adirondack Upland	West Point	Thousand Islands	Henry Hudson
Snapping Turtle	Fort Ticonderoga	Niagara Falls	Franklin Delano Roosevelt	Appalachian Upland

New York Bingo

Giovanni da Verrazano	Appalachian Upland	Fort Ticonderoga	Executive Branch	Thousand Islands
Judicial Branch	Washington Irving	Lake Placid	Ellis Island	Millard Fillmore
Franklin Delano Roosevelt	Coney Island		Apple(s)	United Nations
Henry Hudson	Snapping Turtle	Legislative Branch	Motto	Industry (-ies)
Albany	New England Upland	Lake George	St. Lawrence-Champlain Lowland	Beaver

New York Bingo

Erie Canal	Franklin Delano Roosevelt	Washington Irving	Fort Ticonderoga	Beaver
Buffalo	Great Lakes Plain	Kingston	Legislative Branch	New York City
Atlantic Coastal Plain	Flag		John Jay	Adirondack Upland
River(s)	Martin Van Buren	Theodore Roosevelt	Motto	Snapping Turtle
Statue of Liberty	St. Lawrence-Champlain Lowland	New England Upland	Thousand Islands	Industry (-ies)

New York Bingo: Card No. 20

New York Bingo

Judicial Branch	Appalachian Upland	Kingston	Fort Ticonderoga	River(s)
Atlantic Coastal Plain	Industry (-ies)	Border	Executive Branch	New Netherland
Dairy Products	Lake George		Franklin Delano Roosevelt	Niagara Falls
Legislative Branch	Ellis Island	Snapping Turtle	Hudson Mohawk Lowland	St. Lawrence-Champlain Lowland
John Jay	New England Upland	Beaver	Climate (-ic)	Motto

New York Bingo

Empire State	Henry Hudson	Industry (-ies)	Albany	Cooperstown
New York City	Washington Irving	United Nations	Executive Branch	Apple(s)
Buffalo	Millard Fillmore		New Netherland	Flag
Snapping Turtle	Hudson Mohawk Lowland	Motto	Adirondack Upland	Kingston
New England Upland	Climate (-ic)	Franklin Delano Roosevelt	Dairy Products	John Jay

New York Bingo

Border	Franklin Delano Roosevelt	Ellis Island	Albany	Beaver
Appalachian Upland	Erie Canal	Lake George	Judicial Branch	Adirondack Upland
Henry Hudson	Cooperstown		Theodore Roosevelt	New Netherland
Dairy Products	New England Upland	Snapping Turtle	Climate (-ic)	Motto
River(s)	Martin Van Buren	St. Lawrence-Champlain Lowland	Legislative Branch	Industry (-ies)

New York Bingo

Border	St. Lawrence-Champlain Lowland	Erie Canal	Franklin Delano Roosevelt	Executive Branch
Industry (-ies)	Beaver	Kingston	New York City	New Netherland
Flag	Empire State		Cooperstown	Dairy Products
River(s)	Theodore Roosevelt	Snapping Turtle	Climate (-ic)	Atlantic Coastal Plain
Statue of Liberty	John Jay	New England Upland	Washington Irving	Martin Van Buren

New York Bingo

John Jay	Kingston	Franklin Delano Roosevelt	Niagara Falls	Industry (-ies)
Adirondack Upland	Atlantic Coastal Plain	Judicial Branch	Border	Apple(s)
Hudson Mohawk Lowland	Executive Branch		Theodore Roosevelt	Snapping Turtle
United Nations	River(s)	Martin Van Buren	New England Upland	Millard Fillmore
Beaver	Erie Canal	Buffalo	Constitution	Statue of Liberty

New York Bingo

Industry (-ies)	Franklin Delano Roosevelt	Henry Hudson	New York City	Empire State
Legislative Branch	Washington Irving	Executive Branch	Erie Canal	Border
Hudson Mohawk Lowland	Theodore Roosevelt		Millard Fillmore	John Jay
Climate (-ic)	Albany	River(s)	New England Upland	Snapping Turtle
Flag	Constitution	Niagara Falls	Martin Van Buren	Statue of Liberty

New York Bingo

Henry Hudson	Buffalo	Franklin Delano Roosevelt	Erie Canal	Great Lakes Plain
River(s)	Theodore Roosevelt	Judicial Branch	Snapping Turtle	Apple(s)
West Point	Martin Van Buren		New England Upland	John Jay
Empire State	Appalachian Upland	Kingston	Statue of Liberty	Adirondack Upland
Constitution	Millard Fillmore	Industry (-ies)	United Nations	Flag

New York Bingo

Henry Hudson	Erie Canal	United Nations	Franklin Delano Roosevelt	Border
Great Lakes Plain	Industry (-ies)	Theodore Roosevelt	New York City	Millard Fillmore
Martin Van Buren	Dairy Products		Flag	Legislative Branch
Thousand Islands	Empire State	Lake George	New England Upland	Snapping Turtle
Albany	Hudson River	Constitution	Statue of Liberty	River(s)

New York Bingo: Card No. 28

New York
Bingo

Industry (-ies)	Erie Canal	Empire State	Judicial Branch	Hudson River
Motto	Legislative Branch	Kingston	Flag	United Nations
Hudson Mohawk Lowland	Theodore Roosevelt		Apple(s)	Franklin Delano Roosevelt
Great Lakes Plain	River(s)	Iroquois	New England Upland	Snapping Turtle
Border	Executive Branch	Statue of Liberty	Appalachian Upland	Martin Van Buren

New York Bingo: Card No. 29

New York Bingo

Coney Island	Franklin Delano Roosevelt	New York City	Hudson River	Snapping Turtle
Adirondack Upland	Erie Canal	Henry Hudson	Millard Fillmore	Apple(s)
Hudson Mohawk Lowland	Cooperstown		Flag	Kingston
Statue of Liberty	Appalachian Upland	Albany	New England Upland	Theodore Roosevelt
River(s)	Giovanni da Verrazano	Martin Van Buren	Industry (-ies)	United Nations

New York Bingo: Card No. 30

www.ingramcontent.com/pod-product-compliance
Lightning Source LLC
LaVergne TN
LVHW061338060426
835511LV00014B/1993